THE
INFOGRAPHIC
GUIDE FOR
ENTREPRENEURS

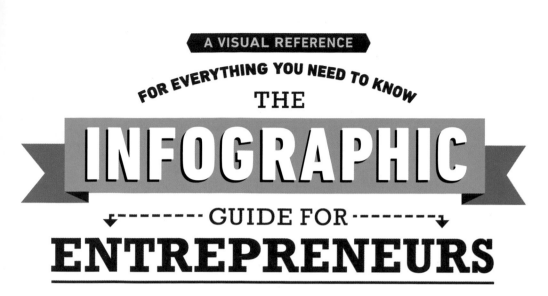

A VISUAL REFERENCE

FOR EVERYTHING YOU NEED TO KNOW

THE

INFOGRAPHIC

GUIDE FOR

ENTREPRENEURS

CARISSA LYTLE and JARA KERN

Adams Media
New York London Toronto Sydney New Delhi

Aadamsmedia

Adams Media
An Imprint of Simon & Schuster, Inc.
100 Technology Center Drive
Stoughton, MA 02072

First Adams Media trade paperback edition February 2019

ADAMS MEDIA and colophon are trademarks of Simon & Schuster.

For information about special discounts for bulk purchases, please contact Simon & Schuster Special Sales at 1-866-506-1949 or business@simonandschuster.com.

The Simon & Schuster Speakers Bureau can bring authors to your live event. For more information or to book an event contact the Simon & Schuster Speakers Bureau at 1-866-248-3049 or visit our website at www.simonspeakers.com.

Interior design by Carissa Lytle at Right Angle Studio, Inc.
Interior images © Shutterstock and Right Angle Studio, Inc.

Manufactured in China

10 9 8 7 6 5

ISBN 978-1-5072-0938-7
ISBN 978-1-5072-0939-4 (ebook)

CONTENTS

GETTING STARTED

BUDGETING & FINANCES

MARKETING & PROMOTION

LIVING YOUR BEST WORK LIFE

RUNNING YOUR BUSINESS

INTRODUCTION

Building a business is one of the most exhilarating, demanding, and complex things you'll ever do in life. You'll utilize the full range of your skillsets, from visioning and planning to crunching numbers and selling your ideas. It requires you to put in an enormous amount of energy, time, and creativity but in return, you get the opportunity to see your dream become reality, and run your business your way.

While there's no shortcut to doing it right, this book offers you tried-and-true advice and pro tips to help get your business off the ground, with fifty colorful, easy-to-reference infographics that provide detailed explanations of the most important concepts in entrepreneurship. Want to know what goes into a vision statement? How to calculate your hourly rate? What sort of contract agreement you've just been handed by your new client? You'll find answers to those questions—and more—in the following pages.

Whether you're looking to launch a coaching business, develop a graphic design agency, or bring your innovative new product to market, this book will offer what you'll need to do it. You'll understand how to structure your business and take advantage of tax deductions. You'll learn how to land your dream clients—and what to do when something goes wrong. You'll find a detailed breakdown on social media channels to help you decide which one is right for promoting your products. And, you'll learn the best ways to balance work and life so that you stay the course—and don't burn out on the way up the mountain.

From bringing your business idea to life through deciding when and if it's time to sell your company, *The Infographic Guide for Entrepreneurs* gives you the best in business education in a fun, easy-to-grasp format.

GETTING STARTED

WHAT KIND OF BUSINESS SHOULD I START?

Now that you're on your way to defining your vision, you'll also need to decide what kind of business you're going to start.

That decision depends on several factors:

FINANCES
Do you have savings? What kind of debt—from student loans to a mortgage or credit card balance—do you carry? Are you able to cover monthly living expenses without steady income? Can you qualify for a loan?

EMPLOYMENT
Are you happy in your job? Do you like your coworkers? Starting a small business while working full time can be challenging, but it can offer you security.

RESOURCES
What resources do you have access to? Mentorship, financing, childcare, and family support all count as resources.

TIME COMMITMENTS
How much time can you devote to your business? Consider your professional, family, volunteer, and social commitments, and factor in time you spend on hobbies. Create a chart to help you visualize it all.

RISK TOLERANCE
What is your level of risk tolerance? Some people feel more comfortable scaling up from freelance to full time, while others jump in feet-first without looking back.

➡ CHOOSE TO START A SIDE HUSTLE IF YOU:

» Plan to use your current income to fund your new venture

» Want to test the waters with your business idea first

» Value your current employment and see your business as a complement

➡ GO FULL TIME IF YOU:

» Are financially and mentally prepared to self-sustain until you're profitable

» Already have a paying client or customer who will provide enough initial revenue

» Are committed to scaling your existing side hustle into a full-time business

→ DID YOU KNOW? ←

Some employers require disclosures for any paid work outside your full-time role. Be sure to consult your employee handbook or ask your HR department.

5 WAYS
TO STRUCTURE MY BIZ

How should you set up your business? Your business structure determines your tax status and can serve as a protective barrier should a legal problem arise.

DID YOU KNOW?

Business structure affects:

Tax liabilities and rates
Legal considerations
Legacy concerns
Risk to personal assets

SOLE PROPRIETORSHIP

In a sole proprietorship, you own and run your business as one person.

- There is no legal distinction between you and your business.
- You are legally accountable for all debts, loans, and losses.
- You receive all profits—and are solely responsible for taxes.

In a sole proprietorship, you may use a business name other than your own legal name. In many states, you'll need to file a DBA—known as a "doing business as" name—in order to accept payment under your business's name.

PARTNERSHIP

A partnership operates much like a sole proprietorship, except that there are at least two owners. Each partner has what's called joint and several liability, which means they are jointly and individually responsible for neglect or misconduct, even if it's committed by another partner.

LIMITED LIABILITY COMPANY (LLC)

An LLC puts a legal barrier between the business and its owner (or owners). For tax purposes, owners are responsible for all taxes (unless they elect to be taxed like a corporation). It's an excellent choice to protect personal assets from potential debts, loans, and losses incurred in a business.

LIMITED LIABILITY PARTNERSHIP (LLP)

In an LLP, partners manage their own business directly under an umbrella structure. Consulting and professional services businesses with equally vested partners often operate as LLPs. Unlike a traditional partnership, partners are not responsible for each other's misconduct or negligence.

S CORPORATION

In an S corp, the business's income or losses are divided among, and passed through to, its shareholders, who report the income (or loss) on their individual tax returns. Like an LLC or LLP, this business structure puts a legal barrier between the business and the shareholders' personal assets.

WHAT'S MY
VISION?

Simply put, your vision is the heart and soul of your business. It defines your overall goals and reflects how you view the world and your business's place in it. It's also critical to all strategic decision-making.

Your vision statement can be as short as a phrase or as long as a paragraph. It should be motivational, which can matter as much to you day to day as it might matter someday to your (eventual) employees.

VISION VS MISSION

You're probably familiar with mission statements. A mission statement answers, **"Why does your company exist?"** while a vision statement is sweeping and forward-looking.

DID YOU KNOW?

Research shows that employees
who consider their company's vision meaningful have
significantly higher engagement levels than those
who don't. Engagement matters—for productivity,
tenure, and ambassadorship.

FOUR STEPS

TO WRITING YOUR VISION STATEMENT

Now that you know why defining your vision is essential to
your success, you can use these steps to actually write it.

Write from the future.
Vision statements are meant to be forward-
looking. Imagine yourself five to ten years in the future
and project what your business will have accomplished.
Use the present tense and concise, clear language.

Define your core values.
What's important to you? How do you see the world?
Your vision statement should reflect your views and values.

Dream big.
A vision statement should be ambitious!
Infuse your statement with passion and emotion.

Ask for feedback.
Everyone has a trusted inner circle. Reach out to
yours for input and direction—and listen carefully
to incorporate what they say.

GET INSPIRED

Feeling stuck? Make a short list of ten brands you admire,
and research their vision statements. You can usually
find them on a website's Company or About page.

MAKING A COMMITMENT

Once you've decided to start your business, you might find your head spinning. It's normal to feel this way—many would-be entrepreneurs are foiled by a lack of confidence, resources, and motivation. **That doesn't have to be you— but success does require honesty.**

Set Expectations
Whether you'll continue to work full time or focus 100% on your new venture, you'll be spending more hours working. Be honest with your spouse or partner, family, and friends so that they understand where your focus is.

Be Disciplined
Take the time to map out your weekly schedule and determine when you'll work. How will you organize your time? What might have to shift?

(AND NOT FREAKING OUT ABOUT IT)

Outsource

What can you take off your plate to free up more time? Small changes—like ordering in one night per week, buying prebagged vegetables, or reducing a current volunteer commitment—can add up.

Put a Timeline in Place

Give yourself a timeline and you might feel more secure. Perhaps you'll spend six months growing your side hustle or plan to break even within nine months. Whatever it is, that timeline can make you feel more comfortable about your commitment.

Set a Date for Your Own Review

You'll be surprised what you discover about your business and your strengths after one year. Put a date on the calendar for your own annual review one year from now.

HELLO
MY NAME IS

?

WHAT'S IN A
NAME?

Before you were born, your parents spent a great deal of time and energy thinking about your name. Why? Because it was going to be the first thing out of your mouth when you introduced yourself—for the rest of your life.

The same thing is true for your business, which is why choosing a name is an important decision. So how do you come up with a great name?

6 STEPS TO NAMING YOUR BUSINESS

1 Decide: are you—or aren't you—the brand?
This is a very big decision. Your name is best suited to be part of your brand if you're offering coaching, consulting, or creative services, and you're the face of the company.

2 Get inspired.
Make a list of the top ten brand names you love. Ask yourself what about those names appeals to you. Then start drafting your own shortlist.

3 Be clear—or you'll need a tagline.
A creative, original name can be an asset—or a deterrent. As a rule of thumb, if your company's name doesn't describe the product or service you offer, you're going to need a tagline or descriptor.

4 Is it in use already?
You'll want to research your shortlist for names already in use. After all, it's a bummer to come up with the perfect name only to find it's already taken. Use InterNIC at www.internic.net/whois.html as a research tool.

5 Determine domain.
Once you've narrowed down your list, you'll want to consider your domain options. Remember that .org is usually reserved for nonprofits and .edu is reserved for educational institutions. For-profit businesses most commonly use .com or .biz.

6 Ask for feedback.
Pay close attention to the emotional feedback your name provokes when you ask your most trusted friends and advisers for their honest opinions.

WHAT MAKES MY BUSINESS UNIQUE?

DEFINING YOUR:

UNIQUE SELLING PROPOSITION

• • •

What is your business's **USP**? Answering that big question is the first step in creating a business that customers genuinely love. After all, you can't be all things to all people—an adage as true in business as in the rest of life.

DID YOU KNOW?

A GOOD USP HELPS YOU:

Stand out from your competition

Create pricing power

Offer products that appeal to your ideal customer

Build customer loyalty

Be memorable

5 TIPS FOR CREATING AN EFFECTIVE USP

Know your customer

Identify and exclusively appeal to your ideal customer. Learn preferences, shopping habits, and purchasing concerns—and factor that information into your planning.

Surprise and delight

Develop a product plus service mindset. Whether yours is a retail, coaching, or creative business, going the extra mile for your customers will build loyalty.

Be personable

People buy things from people. A strong personality can help your business, as long as it aligns with what you're selling.

Be different

Be wary of falling into the "best" trap. Instead of trying to differentiate yourself as the best, focus instead on what makes you different.

Tap the tribe

Learn from your customers by listening, asking for feedback, and iterating to improve.

SETTING UP SHOP

WEBSITE AND E-COMMERCE PLATFORMS

Choosing your digital home is a decision best made wisely. The first—and most important—marketing tool you'll need is a website. **What are your options?**

DIY WEBSITE PLATFORMS

Several existing website platforms offer powerful DIY capabilities and design templates. Most operate on an annual or monthly contract basis, and you can opt to add e-commerce capabilities.

Squarespace

Gain access to a large library of pre-existing templates. Add your content, control colors, and choose fonts, manipulating it all via drag-and-drop.

Weebly

Weebly is a drag-and-drop interface with a guided setup. Choose from existing templates and customize with your own content.

WordPress

Many of the world's biggest companies have built their websites on this platform. Purchase pre-existing themes, which you populate with your content. A web developer can also help you with customization.

Wix

Wix offers several ways to build a website: Wix Artificial Design Intelligence, Wix Editor, and Wix Code. Wield your own design skills or take advantage of *Wix*'s artificial intelligence to create a site quickly.

E-COMMERCE PLATFORMS

Setting up an online shop? You'll need to choose an e-commerce platform. Here are a few of the most popular.

Amazon

When it comes to online shopping, the world's busiest marketplace is the first—and often only—stop for many. Be aware, though, that the platform charges a monthly fee and a per-sale marketplace fee that can average 15%.

In addition, its built-in comparison shopping puts you side-by-side with competition. Since Amazon Prime offers fast shipping for members, you should consider your fulfillment options carefully. In addition, use *Amazon*'s keyword research tool and make use of bullet points in item descriptions.

eBay

eBay offers buying and selling at auction and fixed-price bases for both new and used goods. You control the price and terms, paying an insertion fee per item. You can also establish and brand an *eBay* store, but you do have to handle your own fulfillment (read: shipping).

Etsy

Etsy is a marketplace for independent sellers to promote handmade and one-of-a-kind items. You'll pay a transaction fee of 3.5% per item, and you handle fulfillment. The platform makes tools and dedicated support available to sellers.

Shopify

This e-commerce platform can function alone or integrate with *Amazon* and POS (point-of-sale) tools—meaning you can conduct face-to-face sales and handle payment through your *Shopify* store using the app. You can also use a "buy" button on your website and social channels. A drag-and-drop interface makes setup easy, and the platform offers sales insights and fulfillment options.

#BUSINESSGOALS

S.M.A.R.T. goal setting helps you shape the business that is right for you. It also helps you define what success looks like.

WHAT ARE S.M.A.R.T. GOALS?

The **S.M.A.R.T.** framework
helps you create goals that are:

 Specific

 Measurable

 Attainable

 Realistic

 Timely

SPECIFIC

You're much more likely to achieve a specific goal than a general one. In setting your specific goals, consider: What do I want to accomplish? Why? By when?

MEASURABLE

You should establish how you'll measure success. Ask yourself: How much? How many? How will I know when I've accomplished my goal?

ATTAINABLE

Setting goals helps you foster the mindset to accomplish them. But you need to set goals that you actually can attain, or falling short will discourage you.

REALISTIC

Choose goals that are realistic. You can't expect to make $100,000 in your first month. Additionally, consider setting an A and a B goal—one that is a slam dunk, and one that is a stretch. Celebrating small wins helps you stay motivated.

TIMELY

Your goals should have a specific time frame attached to them, so you're motivated to reach them.

GOAL TYPES

Not all goals need to be financial. Consider:

- **Professional growth**

- **Skill development**

- **Operational efficiency**

- **Increased visibility**

- **Business or partnership expansion**

RISING ABOVE THE COMPETITION

Who is going to be competing with you for customers? Identifying and evaluating your competition goes a long way toward helping you define and refine your critical edge.

AS PART OF CONDUCTING YOUR COMPETITIVE ANALYSIS, YOU'LL WANT TO ANSWER:

» Who is your competition?
» What products or services are they selling?
» What is their current strategy?
» How much are they charging?
» Where are they advertising?

MAKING A COMPETITION GRID

Create a grid to evaluate your competitors for both the opportunity you see and the threats they pose.

1. On the left, list four to five products or services that will compete with yours. To make this easier, you can think about what your customers would buy if your product or service wasn't available.

2. Across the top, list the main features of each product or service, pricing information, and the extent of customer service, support, or guarantees offered.

ASSESSING THE MARKETPLACE

Once you have the competition grid filled out, you should be able to see where your product or service fits into the marketplace.

COWORKING SPACES

AND OTHER ALTERNATIVE OFFICE OPTIONS

Flexible work schedules, the explosion of productivity and collaboration tools, and virtual offices have changed the way many people work— whether they're starting businesses or working in a traditional role.

COWORKING SPACES

Take advantage of office amenities on a subscription or per-use basis. Many workers find the social aspect and potential connections a plus, and also benefit from having access to conference or meeting rooms.

IMPROMPTU WORKSPACES

This is a fancy title for plunking down a laptop at the nearest coffee shop, fast-casual restaurant, or library. Consider the noise level and traffic around you, as well as rules on how long you can occupy a table and when/if it's appropriate to conduct phone calls.

WHAT DO YOU NEED TO BE SUCCESSFUL?

Consider the environment where you do your best work. What will you need?

Social contact?
All the buzz or total quiet?
Meeting or conference space?
Videoconferencing or conference line capabilities?
Collaborative or huddle spaces?
Wireless and BYOD (bring your own device) connectivity?

HOME OFFICE

Working from home delights as many people as it tortures. You cut your commute while multiplying potential distractions. Be disciplined: set aside a workspace and commit to specific office hours.

TRADITIONAL OFFICE

Renting a traditional, fixed office space is an investment—but some entrepreneurs find it the best choice for focused work. Others require a space where they can meet with clients.

BUDGETING & FINANCES

— DID YOU KNOW? —

Online talent marketplaces offer thousands of gig opportunities. Check out *Fiverr*, *LinkedIn ProFinder*, *Thumbtack*, and *Upwork* to get started. Most only charge a fee when you land a gig.

LAUNCHING A SMALL BUSINESS
— IN THE GIG ECONOMY —

Earning in the gig economy is all about identifying opportunities and building the path between now and wow. That takes patience, so keep these tips in mind.

#1 START SOMEWHERE
Your first paying gig or client is a milestone moment. To land it, you might have to offer special pricing or discounts.

#2 BUILD VOLUME
Other clients are more likely to hire you once you have a proven track record with gigs and clients.

#3 UPSELL
Consider offering something to entice clients. For instance, if you're opening a pet-care business, offer a discount on a first dog walk with every three-month subscription purchased. That's an upsell.

#4 EARN REPEAT CLIENTS AND SALES
It's much easier to retain a happy client or customer than to convert a new one. Focus on building a repeat clientele—also called "same-store sales" in the retail biz.

#5 AIM FOR DIVERSIFIED REVENUE
Remember the old saying "Don't put all your eggs in one basket"? Whenever possible, diversify your revenue by considering ways to make dollars for hours, dollars for products or services, and dollars for expertise.

INVESTING IN Y$URSELF

Commanding more money for your time will happen—over time. The best way to ensure your professional growth is to invest in yourself. You'll build your credibility and skills, which will help you offer better products and services to higher-paying customers and clients.

ASSOCIATIONS

Becoming a member of an industry-specific professional association gives you credibility and connections.

CERTIFICATIONS

Earning certifications can help you rise above the competition. Research the professional certifications pertinent to your industry or type of business. Many are offered through online courses.

Best for:

» Coaching

» Consulting

» Professional services

CONFERENCES AND SEMINARS

Attending conferences, seminars, workshops, and other professional in-person events can give you both new information and new contacts for your business.

Research through:

» Professional and trade associations

» Industry-specific websites and journals

ONLINE AND CONTINUING EDUCATION

Keep your skills sharp, stay current, or learn something new with free and paid courses. Browse thousands of choices via:

» Open University on iTunes U

» LinkedIn Learning Courses

» Udemy

» Academic institutions' MOOCs (massive open online courses)

BANK ON IT
BANKING FOR YOUR SMALL BUSINESS

You'll need to decide where to put your hard-earned coin before you start earning. While it can be tempting to deposit your assets directly into your personal bank account, you'll find it safer legally and easier administratively to create a business bank account.

Here's how to choose an institution for your small business banking.

Shop around.
It's worth your time to shop around. Different financial institutions offer different options for small business banking. Call to compare rates, fees, and perks for three to four banks.

Ask about minimum balance.
You'll want to know the minimum balance your bank will require. Can you comfortably meet it? What are you charged if you don't?

DID YOU KNOW? If you set up an entity such as an **LLP**, **LLC**, or **S corp**, you've created a wall between your personal and business assets. To preserve this barrier, you must keep your business funds separate from your personal finances.

OTHER TIPS

✅ Compare fees, which can add up quickly.

✅ Ask about overdraft protection.

✅ Consider deposits: can you use an app? Or do you have to go in person?

Debit or credit?
Having a debit or credit card for your business can greatly simplify tracking your expenses. Ask about applying for a debit or credit card and linking it to your business account.

Have numbers in hand.
Be prepared, even for a phone conversation. Estimate how much revenue your business will generate, as well as what your monthly expenses will be.

Decide how to accept funds.
Credit card, point-of-sale, checks, cash, wire transfers, or direct deposit (ACH)? Banks will want to know how you'll be receiving funds. Be sure you know how you'll get paid before you start your research so you can answer the "how" question. Some banks, for instance, place a limit on the number of wire transfers you're allowed each month.

What's My Cut?

Deciding what to charge stresses many people out. Don't let it. Use the following process to figure out your cut.

STEP 1:
Calculate your expenses

Add up your annual labor and overhead costs:

- Desired (and realistic) annual salary
- Rent, office furniture, and supplies or equipment
- Phone and Internet expenses
- Marketing expenses, like a website, business cards, or advertising
- Professional memberships
- Professional services (accounting, tax prep, lawyers' fees, and more)
- Insurance, permits, and license fees
- Shipping, delivery, and inventory fees
- Fringe benefits, like healthcare, retirement benefits, income taxes, and self-employment taxes

STEP 2:
Choose a profit margin

Remember, you're in business to earn a profit. While there isn't a standard profit margin, 10%–20% is common.

STEP 3:
Determine your billable hours

Factor in:

- Average number of hours you'll work per week
- Weeks you'll work per year (allow for vacation/holiday time)

Anticipate spending 25%–30% of your time on non-billable tasks.

DID YOU KNOW?

You can choose to charge:

- An hourly rate (also called "time and materials")
- A fixed fee for an entire project
- A retainer (a set amount each month)

- On commission
- Via stock, options, or revenue sharing
- A combination of the above

DO THE MATH:

With a two-week vacation, assume you'll work **50 weeks x 40 hours = 2,000 hours a year**.

Figure 30% non-billable time for **2,000 x 0.7 = 1,400 billable hours** worked annually.

STEP 4:
Calculate your hourly rate

Use this formula:

> **(Salary + Overhead) x (100% + Desired Profit Percentage)**
> _____
> **Annual Hours Worked**
>
> **= HOURLY RATE**

STEP 5:
Research your marketplace

You now have an hourly rate! But is it realistic? Determine if you should adjust your rate up or down by:

- Contacting a professional or trade organization to benchmark rates in your field
- Investigating what other professionals charge
- Searching salary rates, comparable for industry and experience, on sites such as:

  www.salary.com
  www.glassdoor.com
  www.payscale.com

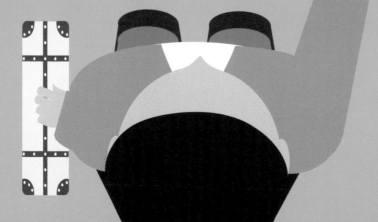

NEGOTIATING LIKE A PRO

If you've ever been offered a job or bought a car, chances are that you've had a taste of negotiation. Sharpening your negotiation skills will benefit both you and your business. Go into every negotiation with a few key points in mind.

1. GOALS

Know what your goals are. Do you want to negotiate a preferential rate with a supplier? Strike up a lucrative long-term agreement? Be sure you've prioritized what's most important to you.

2. ANCHOR

Anchoring is about setting the opening price in a negotiation, and whoever does it can get the upper hand. Should you offer a price or let the other party go first? That's a delicate dance. If you think it'll protect your own interests, you should offer first. If you think the other party's offer will be advantageous, wait.

3. COMPROMISE

Crafting creative solutions with another party can benefit everyone. Be sure you're listening to the other party's goals and priorities and considering them like puzzle pieces alongside yours.

4. BATNA

This stands for "Best Alternative to Negotiated Agreement." You should go into every negotiation with one. Determining what it is—ultimately—is up to you. To determine your BATNA, answer for yourself: "What would I do if I can't come to an agreement?"

Creative ideas for negotiation

Barter

Pro bono work with credit

Part payment, part trade

Revenue share

DID YOU KNOW?

You can—and may be asked to—negotiate on a wide range of things. These include:

- Your fees or hourly rates
- Payment terms
- Office space expenses
- Marketing and advertising
- Service/subscription fees

WRITE-OFFS:
5 TIPS
TO AVOID THE IRS

Let's face it: no one loves paying taxes. You didn't love it when taxes came out of your paycheck, and you're not going to love paying taxes as an entrepreneur.

When you're a small business owner, though, you'll want to make sure you're taking every advantage of your secret weapon: expenses. Here are five expense deductions you should take.

1 Business and professional fees

Anything you pay to someone else in the course of doing business counts as a tax deduction. Did you join a membership association? Pay an accountant? Consult with a lawyer to set up your LLC? All these are deductions for the tax year in which they occurred.

2 Auto and travel expenses

Traveling to conventions, trade shows, or meetings? Your airfare and lodging, as well as 50% of any meals you eat out (whether alone or with clients), are deductible. For instance, if you used your car for business in 2018, you'd be able to deduct up to 54.5 cents per mile driven, as well as tolls and parking fees (the rate is subject to change each year). The IRS can really crack down on business vs. personal car usage, so be sure your recordkeeping is 100% accurate.

3 Phone and Internet

Using your cell phone to conduct business? You can deduct the business-related portion of your monthly bill. As with your auto expenses, you'll want to ensure absolute accuracy in tracking expenses.

4 Software, supplies, and equipment

Your computer, software subscriptions, and other office equipment are fully tax-deductible, so save receipts for your printer cartridges, business card printings, and other such costs. Be sure to take depreciation into account—or the reduction of an asset's value due to its age, obsolescence, or wear and tear.

5 Healthcare

Many healthcare costs are deductible for small business owners, though exactly what is deductible depends on your business structure. For example, if you're a sole proprietor, your premiums are 100% deductible on Form 1040 as an adjustment to income. You might wish to consult a tax accountant for specifics that relate to your business.

ACCOUNTING
— WITHOUT A CPA —

Most entrepreneurs don't have formal training as accountants— and if this is you, **don't lose sleep over it**. The reality is that you can keep your small business accounting simple and effective.

REQUESTING PAYMENT

Retail businesses need to provide receipts to customers at the time of purchase, no matter how you've accepted payment.

Professional services businesses will often invoice clients at the end of a project, a month, or a quarter. To do so, you'll use an invoice. You can find templates in Microsoft Office programs, use a Google Doc, or you can create your own. Invoices must include:

- Invoice date
- Billing and responsible parties' names and information
- Invoice number
- Amount invoiced
- Amount due
- Payment and payable terms (due date and how to pay)

Choose your payment terms:

» **Due upon receipt**

» **Net 15**, which means payment is due within 15 days of the invoice date

» **Net 30**, which means payment is due within 30 days of the invoice date

These dates determine the deadline for payment. Keep in mind your cash flow needs.

ACCEPTING PAYMENT

Will you accept checks? Do you prefer direct deposit or require payment via wire transfer? Will you use Stripe, PayPal, Chase QuickPay, Venmo, or other online payment transfer platforms?

PAYING YOURSELF

If you're a sole proprietorship, LLC member, or LLP partner you simply take your earnings as a draw. There's no need for setting up and submitting payroll. You will have to pay your own payroll taxes on your company's earnings through quarterly estimated tax payments.

If, however, you organize as a corporation, payment will happen via payroll—even if you're paying yourself as the business's only employee. It's best to consult with a tax accountant so you set up payroll properly—and avoid pricey penalties.

TRACKING INCOME & EXPENSES

You can use a simple accounting program—such as QuickBooks or FreshBooks—or you can track income and expenses by creating and managing a Google Sheets or Excel document. To make filing your taxes as easy as possible, stay on top of all income and expenses each month.

CONTRACTS FOR FREELANCERS

It's a smart idea to protect yourself—and your business—by having a contract in place before you begin a project or start on a retainer. You'll also encounter contracts from people and companies you do business with. Here are five of the most common types of contracts.

#1
LETTER OF AGREEMENT

What

Simple letter with easy-to-understand language listing what each party agrees to

When

Use with parties you know and trust

Heads Up

Least legally binding contractual document of them all

#2
NON-DISCLOSURE

What

Guarantees you won't disclose clients' proprietary information (or vice versa)

When

Often used before projects enter sensitive discussions

Heads Up

Respect these—and treat NDA information with the gravity it deserves

#3
NON-COMPETE

What

Asks you to sign away your rights of competition

When

Used by clients to eliminate competition under stipulations of name, geography, and/or time

Heads Up

Vet carefully to ensure you're not agreeing to terms that can limit your business growth

DID YOU KNOW?

You can certainly hire a lawyer to help you create reusable contract templates, but you might be able to access them through professional or association memberships, or online.

#4
STATEMENT OF WORK

What

Lays out the major details of a work arrangement

When

Used by larger clients and companies, or during new or complex projects

Heads Up

Eliminates formal contracts' legal language; ensure details are clear

#5
FORMAL CONTRACT

What

A document used by larger clients and companies

When

Often used by clients for all freelance agreements

Heads Up

Legally binding; review with a lawyer if formal legal language is unclear

HEALTH INSURANCE

Finding affordable health insurance coverage is a daunting task.
Where do you start?

DO I NEED COVERAGE?

Yes, you do. Insurance can protect you from costly illnesses and injuries, and can keep you from owing a lot of money all at once. In some cases, insurance is legally mandated and you may even need to pay a fine for not being covered. Overall, having insurance is a good plan for you and your entrepreneurial goals.

WHY DOES IT COST SO MUCH MORE?

Remember the saying "There's strength in numbers"? As a salaried employee, you paid a premium on your employer's group rate policy. You're now a small shop, or a shop of one, so you don't have that collective buying power or scale anymore.

ENROLL AT THE RIGHT TIME.

Enrollment for a given plan typically begins and ends at the same time each year. You must enroll during this period unless special circumstances apply, such as gaining a dependent through marriage or the birth or adoption of a child.

SHOP AROUND.

Compare plans, rates, and types of coverage using:

- National groups and organizations, such as the Freelancers Union (www .freelancersunion.org)
- Your state's health insurance marketplace (www.healthcare.gov)
- Private insurance plans' individual websites
- Brokers

USE A SUBSIDY IF YOU QUALIFY.

If you make less than $48,560 as an individual or $100,400 for a family of four, you may be eligible for a subsidy or tax credit. Use the Kaiser Family Foundation subsidy calculator: www.kff.org/interactive/subsidy-calculator/.

TAKE THE DEDUCTION.

Many healthcare costs are deductible for small business owners. If you're a sole proprietor or have a single-member LLC, your premiums are 100% deductible on Form 1040 as an adjustment to income. Consult a tax professional for expertise on your specific situation.

FACTOR IN YOUR PREMIUMS AS A COST OF DOING BUSINESS.

This is where you have to get real—really fast. Can you afford the health coverage you need? Factor its cost into your pricing. [For more on calculating your prices, see What's My Cut? in this section.]

WAIT, DO I NEED A LAWYER?

Have you ever heard the old saying **"An ounce of prevention is worth a pound of cure"**? There are many things you'll be able to handle, but for some things you'll want a professional. How do you know when an ounce of prevention is worth a lawyer's fees?

PRO TIP:

Having a lawyer before the need arises could be **one of the smartest business decisions you ever make**. Look for a small business lawyer or ask for a recommendation, and meet with him or her as a get-to-know-you.

Things to handle yourself

- Naming your business
- Buying your domain name
- Creating a single-member LLC
- Applying for your EIN
- Securing business permits
- Hiring employees
- Creating contracts

Things to entrust to a lawyer

- Employee or client/customer lawsuits
- Complaint filings
- Investigations for violations
- Selling your business
- Business acquisitions
- Environmental or legal issues
- Contributing appreciated property to your partnership or LLC

SECTION 3

MARKETING & PROMOTION

WHAT'S IN A BRAND?

branding
FOR BEGINNERS

Many entrepreneurs starting a small business consider a brand and a logo to be the same thing, but they're not.

Simply put, your brand is the idea or image of your company and it's expressed in many ways:

- Business name
- Logo
- Slogan or tagline
- Design
- Messaging and content
- Voice and tone

A consistent brand that delivers value and perpetually delights will help you create a strong following with loyal customers. When you've done that, you'll be well on your way to building a thriving small business.

STEPS TO CREATING YOUR BRAND

STEP 1

Define your message. Simply put, what do you do? And what are the key points you want your customers to know? Focus on distilling your highest-level ideas and values into three to four key points to create a tagline that matches your message.

STEP 2

Integrate and be consistent. Integrating your brand means extending it to details like your email signature, your signage, and even how you answer your phone. Making decisions on all aspects of your brand's expression helps employees carry out consistency for you.

STEP 3

Create your brand voice. If your brand were a person, would he or she be friendly? Cheeky? Elegant? Your brand's personality and voice come through in images, design, and copy.

STEP 4

Be true to your brand. Being true to your brand is about delivering on what you promise your customers. It's about talking the talk and walking the walk, from what you promote to your customer service.

STEP 5

Choose—and use—a great logo. Your logo is your mark, and it should appear on every piece of product, packaging, or promotion that you use. (For more guidance on your logo, see Making Your Mark in this section.)

WHAT'S IN A

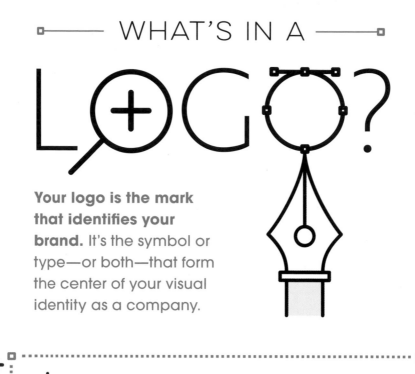

LOGO?

Your logo is the mark that identifies your brand. It's the symbol or type—or both—that form the center of your visual identity as a company.

A SHORT HISTORY OF THE LOGO

The contemporary logo has many ancestors, including:

- Ancient cylinder seals (3300 B.C.E.)
- Coins (600 B.C.E.)
- Coats of arms
- Watermarks
- Royal seals

During the Industrial Revolution in the eighteenth century, photography and lithography—printing—contributed to the rise of an advertising industry that combines type and images together on one page. The result? The poster.

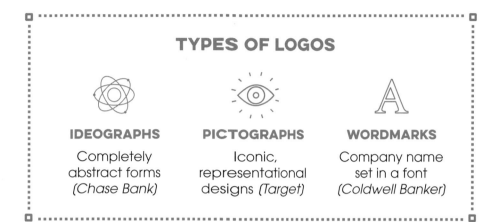

TYPES OF LOGOS

IDEOGRAPHS
Completely
abstract forms
(Chase Bank)

PICTOGRAPHS
Iconic,
representational
designs *(Target)*

WORDMARKS
Company name
set in a font
(Coldwell Banker)

DID YOU KNOW?

Logo is short for **logotype**, which is from the Greek **logos** ("word") and **typos** ("imprint").

TIPS ON MAKING YOUR MARK

+ Hire a graphic designer

+ Be clear on who you are as a company

+ Paint a picture of your target customer

+ Engage in color mapping, or entrust it to your designer

+ Be mindful of usage: social media channels require thumbnails of your logo

+ Commit to your logo; frequent redesign is counterproductive

Working for the right clients makes everyone happy. **So how do you find them?**

Understand whom you'd like to work for—and whom to avoid.

Remember that you can't be all things to all people. What expertise do you have to offer? What kind of work, content, or challenge will you most love?

 Appeal to the right client. Once you know whom you want to work for, go fishing for that client—exclusively. Think about where they are and how to find them: *Facebook, LinkedIn,* trade shows, referrals, and other sources.

 Go on a first date. Make it your rule to interview all potential clients and let them interview you. This can be as simple as a short exploratory phone call. To set expectations and protect your time, cap these at fifteen to twenty minutes.

 Search using keywords. Talent marketplaces—such as *Upwork* and *LinkedIn ProFinder*—let you search jobs and opportunities by specific keywords. You can position your capabilities or filter potential clients using these.

 Set expectations. A huge ingredient in success is making sure you've heard your client and you can deliver what is asked of you (and when). When it's clear who is responsible for what—and by when—you are on the right track.

FINDING & LANDING
YOUR DREAM CLIENTS

Target nearby events.
Donate your product or service to a local fundraiser. Set up a booth at the farmers' market or local festival. Sponsor a local 5K and include a flyer in the race packet. Grassroots promotion can be an inexpensive and effective way of connecting with terrific clients.

Go local.
Many local businesses, libraries, and other community spaces feature areas where you can post a flyer, business card, or pamphlet. Be sure to respect the rules and ask permission if necessary.

Ask for referrals.
Did you build a great client relationship and deliver a stellar project? Way to go! While clients will often refer you naturally, it never hurts to state you're looking for new clients and appreciate being kept in mind.

Take notes and reflect.
Part of your journey as an entrepreneur is learning and improving. Take time to reflect on what works and what doesn't, and let the takeaways inform your approach in the future.

WHAT MAKES A GREAT WEBSITE?

TEN TIPS
TO MAKE A GREAT FIRST IMPRESSION:

1. Choose a website platform

Squarespace, Weebly, Wix, WordPress, and more all offer an array of design templates and easy drag-and-drop content management interfaces.

[For more details on website platforms, see Setting Up Shop in Section 1.]

2. Bake in mobile responsiveness from the start

Keep in mind that the world is mobile, with many people accessing sites from smartphones and tablets. Most website platforms offer mobile responsive design capabilities, but you'll want to be sure to test yours on different mobile devices before you launch.

3. Keep it simple

Your site map should be beautifully simple. For most small businesses, a site map including Home, About, Services or Shop, Blog, and Contact pages is sufficient.

4. Impress on the homepage

The point of your homepage is to introduce your company and your unique value in customer-focused, benefit-oriented language. Your homepage content determines if people go further into your site, so be bold, splashy, and clear.

5. Rock your About page

Your About page is the second-most-visited page. Here is where your storytelling should shine. Why were you founded? What's your mission?

6. Incorporate a call-to-action

What do you want your customers to do? Buy your product? Contact you about your consulting services? Be sure you're asking them to take action—and be consistent on each page.

7. Put your logo front and center

Use it in a header on your homepage and ensure that it's in the upper left or right corner of each page on your site. You might also consider placing it in your footer.

8. Use beautiful imagery

Stunning on-brand imagery works wonders in wowing your customers. Consider large, horizontal images for "hero" images on your homepage and other pages, and smaller images—headshots, action or team shots, and product pictures—sprinkled throughout your site.

9. Go easy on the copy

Remember that people have short attention spans. Go light on the copy, with just enough information for people to understand your value and difference.

10. Make it easy for customers to contact you

Put your phone number and email where customers will easily find them. Better yet, integrate automatic calling and a hyperlinked email so your customers can strike while the iron is hot. Put your social media links front and center as well, so your customers can see what you're up to and share this info on their own pages, which will, in turn, help you grow your following.

SELL YOURSELF

WITHOUT SELLING OUT

Every job, in some way, is a sales job.
What makes sales feel good and not like selling out?

THINK VALUE, NOT SALES

When you offer value, people buy it. Reframe your thinking and shift your vocabulary so that you're not selling something, you're delivering value.

CREATE—AND REFINE— YOUR ELEVATOR PITCH

You'll be asked it a million times—by clients, at networking events, and even family parties: "So, what do you do?" Now is the time to deliver your elevator pitch.

CONNECT WITH YOUR CUSTOMERS

Simply put, people buy things from people. Building relationships with your customers or clients creates loyalty.

UNDERSTAND YOUR CUSTOMER'S NEEDS

When you know your customer's pain point— the thing he or she needs to solve—you speak to that with your sales pitch.

3 STEPS TO A PERFECT PITCH

An elevator pitch is the thirty-second answer to the "What do you do?" question. It's so named because delivering it should take you the length of an elevator ride.

These three prompts will help you write your pitch:

1

"Did you know…" engages your audience and frames the problem you solve

2

"What I do…" explains what you offer and how you do it

3

"So that…" expresses the benefit(s) of your service or product

SEE IT IN ACTION

The inventor of Goodr sunglasses, made for runners, cyclists, and triathletes, might use this pitch: *"Do you know how hard it is to find inexpensive athletic sunglasses that stay on your face? What we did is invent the best polarized, no-bounce glasses on the market for under $30, so that athletes can perform well without spending big bucks."*

PRACTICE, PRACTICE, PRACTICE

Practice your new pitch on your family, friends, and colleagues. When you're confident in your abilities and expertise, and you have the elevator pitch that conveys it, sales will come naturally.

Be active on Twitter

Rich in industry information and flat in hierarchy, *Twitter* is a goldmine for any entrepreneur. It also gives you access—without layers—to some of the biggest and brightest stars in your industry. Invest the time in *Twitter* and you'll reap the rewards of connection.

How to Network
(without networking)

Networking leads to connections, which can lead to mentorships, clients, and business opportunities.

Use these tips to stop thinking of it as networking and start thinking of it as connecting.

Go to or organize a meet-up

Search for local chapters relevant to your industry—Northwest Chicago Female Entrepreneurs, anyone?—or start up one of your own to attract new connections with common interests and goals.

Join a professional membership or association

In-person events and member directories give you ample opportunities to connect with potential mentors, collaborators, or clients.

Be active on LinkedIn

The same is true for *LinkedIn*, and it's far less crowded. Be sure to optimize your profile with a good headshot and summary, and take advantage of the site's ability to find connections via your email list. Aim to post a piece of industry news four to five times per week and follow people you admire.

Attend a conference or seminar

Bring your business cards, your smile, and your elevator pitch—and head home with a handful of new connections. As a plus, you'll also fill your brain with new ideas and knowledge.

Ask for connections

This is not the time to be shy. Reach out to your inner circle of friends, colleagues, and mentors, and ask if they can recommend someone who might be a good connection for you. Following up on that connection could take the shape of a short phone call or an in-person coffee meeting. It goes without saying that you should be the person buying that coffee when someone gives you his or her time.

Attend alumni events in your city

Whatever college or university you attended, it probably has a local alumni chapter active in your city. Mixing and mingling with fellow Badgers, Cornhuskers, or Buckeyes gives you new contacts with a shared history.

BEING SOCIAL:

WHICH CHANNELS SHOULD I USE?

The numbers don't lie—**social media is one of your best options for building your business.**

The average American spends two **hours per day on social media**

Facebook **is the second-most popular site in the world (behind** *Google***)**

36% of Americans ages 18-29 are on *Twitter*

Social media strengthens your brand by helping you:

➜ Build relationships

➜ Provide better customer service

➜ Gain insight and fast feedback

➜ Access industry information and influencers

DID YOU KNOW?

But where is your time and effort best spent? **Use this handy chart to decide.**

	facebook		*Instagram*
Best for	Lifestyle, personal, and consumer-oriented brands	Almost everyone	Lifestyle and personal brands
Type of content	Multimedia	280 characters of almost anything	Images and videos
Post frequency	1–2/day	7+/day	1–3/day

	Linked in.	▶ **YouTube**	ⓟ **Pinterest**
Best for	Professionals and professional services	Lifestyle, personal, consumer-oriented, and niche brands	Lifestyle and personal brands
Type of content	Industry news, updates, and long-form blogs	Videos	Images
Post frequency	1/day	Varies	Link out to your content

Blogging, Vlogging, AND Podcasting

Content marketing drives the digital world. If you're looking to build your audience, there is no better way to do it than creating and promoting high-quality content. What are your options?

BLOGGING

Short for "weblogging," blogging has been around for more than twenty years. Blogging refers to regularly writing and sharing fresh content on your site (filled with pictures and links, of course). Aim for at least 400 words—longer if you like—and posting at least once per month. Work ahead so you have a bank of content ready in advance.

Promote via:

- Your own website
- Your own social channels
- Other sites and social channels
- Email
- LinkedIn Publishing for pieces with 1,500+ words

VLOGGING

Vlogging is the video version of blogging—sharing regular video updates covering topics of interest pertinent to your brand. Think bite-sized in length and strive for originality and personality to stand out.

Promote via:

- *YouTube*
- Your own website
- Your own social channels
- Email
- Other sites and social channels

PODCASTING

Podcasts connect you with listeners on the go and are easy to record using your smartphone's built-in microphone. Aim for episodes of fifteen to sixty minutes and create an outline or a script to stay focused. Be sure to take advantage of the "show notes" section and mention your own site and social media in the recording itself.

Promote via:

- iTunes and Google Play stores
- Your own website
- Your own social channels
- Email
- Other sites and social channels

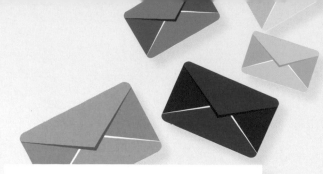

LET'S KEEP IN TOUCH

TOP EMAIL MARKETING TIPS

Your email list will become one of your business's most valuable assets. It's where you will build awareness and loyalty and drive conversions. Use these tips to make email marketing work for you.

CHOOSE AN EMAIL SERVICE PROVIDER (ESP)

An email service provider gives you a tool to set up polished emails and get insights into who is opening and reading your content. ESPs also give you drag-and-drop building capabilities, images, and troubleshooting advice. Mailchimp and Constant Contact are two popular choices.

Did You Know?
ESPs are serious about spam. You'll need to affirm your subscribers have given you permission to email them. If you violate this, you could be blacklisted.

CREATE MEANINGFUL CONTENT

Think blogs, videos, GIFs, and images, and consider your list a platform to offer expertise and insight.

DECIDE ON A FREQUENCY YOU CAN MANAGE

Be realistic. Can you manage an email a week, or is one per month more feasible? Choose a schedule and commit to it.

Build your content in advance. Scrambling each week or month to create your email creates unnecessary stress. Collect ideas, write your emails, and schedule them in advance for smooth sailing.

USE OPT-INS TO BUILD YOUR LIST

This valuable, meaningful content? Don't give it away for free. Provide it in exchange for subscribership; so ask for an email in return for your goodies. Use opt-in tools on your website, as well as on your social media.

MAKE AUTOMATION WORK FOR YOU

Did someone sign up for your email list? Strike while the iron is hot. Have a welcome message delivered automatically by using the features provided by your ESP.

KEEP EMAILS SHORT AND SWEET

Think bite-sized content. Most people read emails on mobile devices, and your emails should take thirty to fifty seconds to read. Write smart, intriguing subject lines and a short and snappy preheader (the text that shows up in the preview mode on a mobile device).

INCLUDE A CALL-TO-ACTION (CTA)

Every email should close with what you want your readers to do: Schedule a call with you? Visit your site? Buy a product? Keep your CTA consistent and always include a link.

Getting Repeat Clients

AND

Making the Most of Referrals

Repeat clients earn you more for your time—it's that simple. Think of it: every new client comes with an acquisition cost—factor in the advertising cost it took to find the client, as well as the fees you've forgone in the process of landing that client.

Additional projects

The fastest way to get repeat clients? Earning multiple projects from the same client. Make sure every new client understands the full range of what you offer. Your website and sales pitch need to make that clear.

The upsell

Sometimes a client starts small, and then you find an opportunity to upsell. Perhaps you rewrite a brochure and then land the website rewrite. Maybe you offer health coaching to one person but can upsell to a couple's package.

The "keep-warm"

Make it a point to stay in front of your clients even after the work has ended. That's where regular email marketing and your social media strategy come in.

The big client

Bigger clients offer you more project opportunities. If you're working with one department in an organization, help your (happy) client refer you to internal colleagues.

The retainer

A good client can become a great client when you're asked to work on retainer. This simply means the client "retains" a portion of your time. Negotiate terms that work for you both, put them in writing, and revisit them regularly.

Referrals—

recommendations and word-of-mouth—are a small businessperson's best friend. They're the most inexpensive and valuable way to land clients just like the ones you love. To encourage them, you should:

Ask your client to consider referring you at the successful conclusion of a project

When appropriate, offer incentives for referrals— discounts, early access, and more

Consider returning the favor when the opportunity arises

Related to referrals, **testimonials** are written kudos that you can use to seal the deal with your marketing. Ask for them—and ask for permission to use them on your website, in your emails, and in your social media.

SECTION 4

LIVING YOUR BEST WORK LIFE

A SOLOPRENEUR'S GUIDE

TO NOT GOING

NUTS

As an entrepreneur, you're going to be wearing more hats than you can count. And you'll switch them all day long. **What can you do to manage stress and remain calm, cool, and collected?**

TAKE BREAKS

Humans are amazing, but we're also, well, human. With all that you'll be juggling, you need to ensure you take time to reset between meetings and intense work sessions.

FIND YOUR PEOPLE

You might find that life as a business owner can be lonely. Keep in touch with your network and inner circle for reasons both professional and social.

BE RESILIENT

Resilience is about refusing to let failure—no matter how big or small—get you down. You're going to need it to stay the course.

TAKE CARE OF YOURSELF

Sleep is necessary downtime for the human brain. Don't forgo it. The same goes for food and exercise.

COMMIT TO A SCHEDULE

Many people need the discipline of a schedule to maximize productivity. This is especially true if you'll be transitioning from a busy, social, deadline-driven work environment to a vast sea of unstructured time as you build your business. Give yourself disciplined yet realistic office hours. Set an end time. And be sure to make time for hobbies, interests, and other commitments.

FIND A MENTOR

Someone who has been successful in building his or her business can prove a valuable connection for you, offering advice, encouragement, and support when you need it most. If you have the resources and think you'll need the accountability, you can also hire a business coach.

DID YOU KNOW?

Multitasking **reduces productivity** and can **increase stress**. That's because the human brain has to constantly stop and start to process multiple actions at once. Be intentional in reducing stimulation and focusing on a single priority at a time.

HOME OFFICE

• • •

Where Does Work End and Life Begin?

When you run your business from home, it's easy to get sucked into never really leaving work. Resist that tendency by setting—and maintaining— ground rules that work for you. After all, you run your business—don't let it run you.

Decide what work/life balance means

Develop clarity on what work/life balance means for you. Does it look like a traditional 9-to-5? Is it part time? What are the needs of your business, finances, and other life commitments?

Create—and stick to—a schedule

How many hours will you work? When will you start? What time will you wrap up? When do you stop checking email each night? What's your end-of-day routine? Consistency is key to success, and a consistent schedule creates discipline.

Set physical boundaries

Out of sight, out of mind. Make sure you are working at home, not living in your office. If you have the space, carve out a dedicated work area. Otherwise, put your laptop away at the end of the day so you can transition to home mode.

Coordinate, coordinate, coordinate

Whether you're part of a family unit or a happily social singleton, being a good human being means coordinating your new schedule with loved ones. Continue to give important relationships the attention they deserve.

Set client boundaries

Again, you're running your business. If you're not willing to take client calls in the evening or over the weekend, don't. You're responsible for setting and defending your own boundaries.

PRO TIP

The flexibility of working from home can help you adjust your schedule to accommodate your most productive hours. If you're an early bird, start work early to take advantage of a peak in energy. If you're a night owl, feel free to shift work to later in the day—when it works for your customers and your friends and family.

TAKING TIME

Most workers, whether they're salaried employees or entrepreneurs, are terrible at taking time off. In fact, most of us take just half our allotted personal time each year. As a business owner, you'll be tempted to forgo downtime—necessary or otherwise.

VACATIONS

Vacations offer the opportunity to travel, recharge, and make memories with loved ones. Don't skip them!

Keep these tips in mind:

» As the person in charge, you don't need to request vacation time. Own it!

» Don't feel ashamed, and don't lie. Let clients and customers know you're taking time off.

» Go with the flow. If you feel like working a bit, do. A change of scenery can spark new ideas.

» Expect to keep a toe in the water—from lightly checking email, to talking to new potential contacts.

PARENTAL LEAVE

When you're self-employed, it can be difficult financially and logistically to take time off with your new baby.

Consider:

» Saving aggressively in advance to give yourself time off.

» Maintaining current commitments, but freezing new projects or clients.

» Subcontracting some work to trusted colleagues (be sure to set expectations).

» Notifying clients so they can plan for your absence.

» Enlisting help from family, friends, or paid sitters.

SICK DAYS

When you're sick, you'll have to decide whether you can tough it out or it's time to take some time. Be transparent with customers—we all get sick. If you're contagious, cancel or reschedule meetings, sales calls, or events where you'll have physical contact with others.

And it's healthy to recognize we all need mental health days from time to time in order to do our best work—and stay the course.

5 TIPS
on Creating a **Winning** Proposal

Proposals are a key part of winning clients and projects.

PRO TIP
Follow up with your client forty-eight hours after sending the proposal, and again a week later if you've heard nothing.

Stand out from the competition with these tips.

1 ### Create a reusable template
Look polished by creating a document featuring your logo, headline and body fonts, and a footer with your contact information (email, website URL, phone number). To preserve its look, make it into a PDF before you send it off.

2 ### Use an opportunity statement
Leading with a vision sets the tone. State in two to three sentences the opportunity you see and what you look forward to assisting the client with.

3 ### Scope deliverables
Proposals tell your clients what they'll pay for and what they'll get. Clearly state deliverables and associated pricing, and get really specific. How many rounds of revision? How will you deliver the final files?

4 ### Include an expiration date
Imagine a situation in which you've sent out six proposals (!) and everyone says "Yes!" at once! You'll be flooded with new work. While that's grand, it's also stressful. Include a date by which clients should agree to terms for specified deliverables.

5 ### Don't forget the fine print
Will your client pay a deposit to begin the engagement? When is that due? What is your hourly rate for work beyond the proposal's scope? What are your rights if the client terminates the engagement? Put your lawyer's hat on and get specific with the terms of your proposal. It's fine to include them in the fine print at the bottom.

HAPPY CLIENTS = HAPPY FREELANCERS

ENSURE YOU'RE A FIT

Can you deliver what your client is looking for? It's important to weed out right away what you can and can't contribute. Decide if you're interested in the client's project and if he or she will make a good collaborator going forward.

LISTEN CAREFULLY

Ensure you understand exactly what your client needs, what the project entails, what resources you'll have access to, and when you need to finish.

PRO TIP

Upset about a client email or call? Don't be reactive and don't react rashly. Take a deep breath, restrain yourself from replying right away, and be sure you're calm enough to respond with equanimity before you do.

BE RESPONSIVE

It's okay to not have an answer right away, but do reply to emails in a timely manner, even if it's to indicate you've registered the request and will be back in touch. Then be sure to follow through.

We've all had the feeling of clicking with colleagues—
and the magic that happens at work afterward.
You can have that same feeling with your clients.

**Be awesome and they will
come back again and again.**

LEARN HOW THEY PREFER TO COMMUNICATE

Some clients love email. Others prefer phone calls or in-person meetings. Still others like dashing off a fast text. Be flexible and adapt to each client's preferred method of contact.

SET EXPECTATIONS

Clearly communicate which are your responsibilities and which belong to your client. Put it in writing in an email and gently follow up. Some people are very prompt, while others are not—and you'll need to protect yourself if your client is not.

DELIVER ON TIME

Be honest about when your client can expect the draft, revision, or final project. Life throws curveballs at all of us from time to time—if you're on the receiving end of one, be transparent about missing the deadline. Then be sure to set a new one and meet it.

MAKING IT RIGHT

WHEN SOMETHING GOES WRONG

Mistakes happen. And eventually one is bound to happen to you. Whether you miss a detail or a deadline, deliver the wrong project, or encounter a difficult client, it's important to know what to do to make it right.

THE UPSET CLIENT

You'll deliver what you think is exactly what the client wanted, and then you'll get a frustrated email or phone call. You'll correct your mistake, and the client still won't like it. Stirred up, he or she will take out their frustration on you.

WHAT TO DO

→ Listen dispassionately.

→ Apologize when necessary.

→ Offer a solution that will work for you both. Can you revise the original? Ask for additional input?

THE POOR REVIEW

You'll receive a bad review with a poor rating—right on your talent marketplace or *LinkedIn* profile for all the world to see.

WHAT TO DO

→ Reach out to the client and offer to correct the work.

→ Explain that your business thrives on reviews, and you're committed to a good experience.

→ Analyze what happened and correct course in your process.

→ Ensure that your next projects are flawless so that the negative review works its way down the profile view.

PRO TIPS

✓ **Develop and cultivate a positive customer service mindset.**

✓ **Whenever possible, put the terms of your deliverable, process, and payment in writing.**

✓ **When committing to due dates, ensure that the client is also committed to his or her side of the equation—and, if not, that your date will shift.**

THE "OOPS, I JUST CAUGHT IT NOW"

You went over your work with a fine-toothed comb—you even had your good friend proofread—and you still didn't catch the misspelling that went out, in the headline no less.

WHAT TO DO

→ Don't sit on the mistake. Reach out right away with an apology and a corrected file.

→ Learn from your mistake and put a process into place so it won't happen again.

DRY SPELLS

Let's face it: dry spells are scary. And they happen to everyone. When you're first starting out, you won't be able to see any seasonality in your year and every dry spell will jangle you.

Keep everything in perspective and learn how to stay afloat during these downtimes.

Common reasons for dry spells:

▸ Loss of project or client

▸ Holidays, spring break, or summer vacation

▸ Longer-than-expected wait for assets, materials, or inventory

▸ Reduction in business development efforts (you've been focused elsewhere)

WHAT YOU CAN DO:

Save aggressively.
This advice is as valuable professionally as it is personally. A cushion can help reduce the anxiety a dry spell causes.

Welcome the slower pace to network and plan.
The connections you make today can yield future work.

Shift your mindset.
Reframe this slow time as the calm before the next storm.

Invest in yourself.
Now is the time to write content, refine your process, or organize your receipts for tax filing. Or maybe you'll invest the time in researching a new product or service, or refreshing your website copy.

Backfill.
Use this time to get ahead on another project you might have otherwise put off.

Keep your good clients warm.
Drop your best clients a line with a new idea or an industry article or blog you think they should read. While overtly fishing for new work is never advisable, staying in front of people works wonders.

Track dry and busy spells.
When you do, you'll be able to detect patterns—so you'll know next year that you're not going out of business, it's just the Christmas shutdown.

EXIT STRATEGIES

CLOSING UP SHOP, PAUSING, OR SELLING

At this point, your exit strategy may be the furthest thing from your mind. After all, you haven't even gotten off the ground. Yet it's wise to think through your options and revisit them regularly should a situation arise in which you'll sell or close your business.

REASONS FOR CLOSING OR SELLING:

- Received a great offer
- Retirement
- Partnership disputes
- Illness or death
- Burnout
- Career change or other transition

PRO TIP

Carefully manage communication regarding the state of your business. Inform customers, vendors, and partners promptly. Ensure payments you're owed are paid and that bills you owe are also taken care of.

SELLING

Should you choose to sell, keep these guidelines in mind:

1. **Be clear on why you're selling.** It's the first thing a potential buyer will want to know.

2. **Prepare well ahead of time.** Doing so a year or more in advance helps you improve your financial records and strengthen your customer base, which can help you attract a higher offer for your business.

3. **Determine its worth.** Get a valuation with a business appraiser so you price your business just right. This document can make your price more credible.

4. **Decide if you'll use a broker.** If you're selling your business to a trusted family member, friend, or associate, you can probably handle the sale yourself and save a broker's commission. If not, you'll likely find the fee money well spent.

5. **Create documentation.** Gather your financial statements and tax returns for the last three to four years; prepare a list of equipment and assets; and include a list of current customer and vendor contacts. Offer these documents to your most qualified buyers.

6. **Make a plan for the profits.** You'll want to consult with a tax accountant or attorney on handling the profits from the sale of your business to avoid unnecessary penalties.

CLOSING

From time to time, entrepreneurs are presented an opportunity too good to pass up. Or, family or financial reasons alter your life circumstances. If—or when—you decide to close your business, communication is key. Tell your customers, partners, and vendors your news, and keep it short and factual. You can also consider whether parking your business on the side or subcontracting your work out temporarily gives you a better option to exit.

THE
ANNUAL REVIEW

Many entrepreneurs and solopreneurs are too busy keeping up with daily business to take time to reflect on the year past and set goals for the year ahead. But if you've made it this far, congrats—this won't be you.

DID YOU KNOW?

Setting aside time to reflect and retool can help you:

+ Find renewed commitment

+ Boost motivation—for you, or perhaps for your team

+ Define key priorities for your business's next phase

+ Refine your messaging

+ Better understand your customers and their needs

+ Identify key weaknesses and make a plan to address them

Your Self-Review in 5 Steps

Conducting your own annual review requires only your honesty in assessment. Start by setting aside some focused time. This might be as short as an afternoon or as long as a day.

1. **Inventory your work.** What did you spend your time on this year? Tally up what your output was, by category if possible.

2. **Attach data on performance.** Which project or product was a home run? What got the best reviews? Looking at your output with success measures in place helps you focus on what you did best.

3. **Look at your business's health.** Consider key metrics, including the number of email subscribers you have, your following on your social channels, your site visitors, your conversions, your revenue, and your profit. Tracking this data year over year can also help you see your business grow.

4. **Determine where you spent your time.** In addition to your output, where did you spend time? How much? Are you spending a lot of time traveling? Are certain administrative tasks taking up a lot of time?

5. **Reflect on what went well and what you can improve.** Honesty in steps 1 through 4 will help you quickly realize where you can be more efficient and effective in the next year. In addition, take time to articulate—and write down—your big goals. After all, we measure what matters.

Take advantage of online tutorials

The Internet offers an almost never-ending array of DIY education options. Immerse yourself in them. Learn how to build websites, or become skilled in a new email service provider platform. Try making images for your social media with tools like Canva, Fotor, or Gravit.

Keep your fingers on the industry pulse

Stay curious and thirsty for knowledge. Follow influencers and thought leaders on social media, especially *LinkedIn*. Stay tuned to your industry news through membership in a professional association, by reading industry content and publications, and by attending key events.

NEVER STOP LEARNING

TRAINING AND CONTINUING EDUCATION

PRO TIP

You're not only learning; you're also investing in yourself. Remember that the fees you pay for training, conferences, and certifications are considered business expenses—so be sure you take advantage of them as tax deductions.

We are living in an incredible era of seismic and disruptive change. Technology is bringing new efficiency and possibility to almost every industry, from the cars we drive to the tools we use for communication and collaboration. What's a good entrepreneur to do?

Get current on new technology
New software or tool? Make sure you know its features and performance inside and out. Take full advantage of its online resources and customer service options.

Get certified
Certain certification programs can set you apart as a professional. From in-person to online training, you often have options on how to pursue credentials that bolster your credibility.

Go back to school
Maybe you'll decide that the time is right to pursue a graduate degree. Consider your options for online or part-time learning programs to figure out the best way to blend education and business.

SECTION 5

RUNNING YOUR BUSINESS

TIME MANAGEMENT

HOW TO MAKE THE MOST OF YOUR DAY

When it comes to productivity, it's important to know what kind of person you are. Are you a motivated self-starter? Or do you need some accountability and time pressure? Knowing what you require to do your best work is half the battle.

Whatever your strengths or needs, make the most of your time with some tested tips.

DOs

DO conclude each day by making a list of tomorrow's to-dos and priorities. You'll save time knowing how to pick up where you've left off.

DO put first things first: concentrate on the day's biggest task first, when you're likely to have the most energy and concentration.

DO checkpoint your to-do list by evaluating where you are and reprioritizing midmorning, midday, and midafternoon.

DO carve out head-down time for yourself. Put your phone on silent and place it across the room.

DO leave yourself a short buffer in between meetings and calls so you're not rushing from one thing to the next.

DO learn where you do your best work. Difficult project? Need the pressure of eyeballs? Take yourself to the library or Starbucks with the commitment that you'll meet a certain milestone.

DON'Ts

DON'T check email reactively. Instead, check email in between tasks, focused time, or meetings.

DON'T sprinkle meetings throughout your day. Divide your time into meeting time, work time, and administrative time for maximum productivity.

DON'T skip meals or sleep—be sure to fuel yourself properly for your best work.

DON'T be unrealistic about how long it will take to do something. Make sure you set aside enough time for each project or task.

DON'T wait until you start a project to make sure you have everything you need to be successful.

DON'T send work rushed or late at night—leave yourself time to look at it with fresh eyes and make sure it represents your best effort.

TECHNOLOGY & EQUIPMENT:

HOW MUCH IS JUST RIGHT?

Different types of businesses require different types of equipment, in addition to any equipment necessary for the work, like landscaping tools, screen-printing machines, cleaning materials, and so on. Carefully assess your needs and start-up costs with these tips on technology and equipment.

COMPUTER EQUIPMENT

Does your business depend on a digital product? Will you be presenting material in person? Many designers, consultants, and coaches rely on a laptop or desktop as the main tool of their businesses. Consider the software you'll be using, as well as the frequency of your travel and presentations, to determine what features are most important and if you need an upgrade. Also consider the type of printer you may need. Designers, photographers, and others in creative services often require higher-quality printing capabilities.

ADMINISTRATIVE TOOLS

G Suite (formerly Google Apps for Work), Office 365, and similar products give you powerful capabilities at reasonable price points. Consider an email skinned to match your website URL for a seamless brand experience. Add in the functionality you need, including calendar software, file sharing, and more.

DISPLAY AND PROMOTIONAL EQUIPMENT

If you're putting on events, attending trade shows, or featuring your business at local events, you'll need to consider opportunities for promotion via signage, booth materials, or other graphics. Consider some under-the-radar reconnaissance at relevant events ahead of time so you can decide how little (or how much) equipment you'll need.

POINT-OF-SALE AND E-COMMERCE EQUIPMENT

Will you be selling products? Whether you do so in-person or online, you'll need something to handle your sales and collect relevant information. A customer relationship management (CRM) and point-of-sale (POS) device can capture customer information and accept payments. Clover, Square, and the *Shopify* platform all offer easy ways of accepting credit card payments.

PRO TIPS

Start lean and scale up. It's easy to get carried away, but it's better to understand what you— and your customers— really need.

Ensure you're accounting for depreciation on assets used for multiple tax years—such as your laptop, extra monitor, point-of-sale tools, and more.

MEETING WITH CLIENTS

IRL AND VIRTUAL RELATIONSHIP BUILDING

Building strong relationships with your clients creates loyalty, which brings more security and prosperity to your business. Ensure you start off and stay on the right foot with clients whether you're meeting in person, by phone, or via videoconferencing with Zoom, Skype, or Slack.

BEFORE THE MEETING

» Set a date, time, and place for the meeting that works for all parties.

» Send a calendar invite with all the meeting details and an alert or reminder built in.

» Send an agenda that clearly outlines your expectations and discussion points.

» If you're presenting, confirm technology and equipment needs so you have what you require to be successful.

DURING THE VIRTUAL MEETING

» Dial in or log in five minutes before anyone else.

» If you're using videoconferencing, dress professionally, choose an appropriate backdrop, and minimize background noise. Make eye contact with the camera on your computer, not the screen (or you'll look like you're looking down).

» Screensharing? Make sure your desktop is clear so you're not showing a document you ought not to.

DURING THE IN-PERSON MEETING

» Leave fifteen to thirty minutes for extra travel time so you avoid the panic of traffic and other unanticipated delays.

» Meeting at Starbucks, Panera, or another restaurant? Plan to get there first so you can secure a table.

» Meeting at an office? You never know what security entails. Make sure you bring your government-issued ID or driver's license.

» Bring copies of the agenda and any other meeting materials.

» Make sure you have ample time and support to set up your technology.

» Greet everyone with a firm handshake and eye contact.

» Thank your clients for hosting you.

» Leave ample time for discussion and reviewing the next steps at the end.

» Respect everyone's time—and conclude on time.

AFTER THE MEETING

» Follow up via email to emphasize the next steps.

Getting Paid:

A STEP-BY-STEP GUIDE

STEP 1: Decide how you'll bill
Will you ask for prepayment?
Bill every month for hours spent?
Or use progress billing—50% down,
50% at conclusion? Decide on how,
and make sure your customer or
client knows and agrees.

**STEP 2: Complete any
forms or setup required**
Does the client require a vendor
agreement or PO? Ensure
you've completed whatever
paperwork is required in order
to be paid on time.

STEP 3: Create an invoice
You can use a template or create
your own. Be sure to include the
date and an invoice number, as
well as the contact information
and name of the responsible
parties. Include fees and a
description of the product or
service rendered, as well as the
total due.

STEP 4: Include terms
Terms refer to when payment is due.
Is your invoice due upon receipt,
meaning your customer needs to
pay right away? Net 15 or Net 30,
which means the payment is due
fifteen or thirty days after the
invoice date? Make sure you take into
account your own cash flow needs
when deciding on invoice terms.

**STEP 5: Track accounts
receivable**
You can use FreshBooks or
QuickBooks, or you can use a simple
Excel or Google Sheets setup. It all
depends on your business volume
and organizational acumen. Keep
track of all open invoices—your
accounts receivable (the fees you're
due).

Yay, it's payday! What does that mean, and how do you get your hard-earned coin?

STEP 6: Accept payment

Cash, check, direct deposit, or ACH? Funds transferred via Chase QuickPay, PayPal, or Venmo? However you accept funds, be sure you're already set up so that your customer can pay your invoice quickly and easily.

STEP 7: Maintain accurate accounting

When an invoice is paid, make sure you track that in your system. After all, it's embarrassing to ask about a payment that's already been made!

Unpaid Invoices and Collections

Occasionally, someone is slow to pay or becomes a delinquent customer. What can you do?

- Follow up—and don't feel like a nag.

- Issue a "second notice" invoice.

- Consider an alternative pay schedule to accommodate your client and be paid in full.

- Engage a collections agency if you're owed at least $50, your invoice is still unpaid ninety days after the due date, and you're not able to work out terms. Understand that the collections agency may charge 15%-25% of the total amount collected, and they may not be able to collect in full.

HIRING YOUR SQUAD

So you need some helping hands. Spend time carefully defining what your staff will do and how many hours they'll spend doing it to help the interviewing and hiring process go smoothly.

FINDING YOUR PEOPLE POWER

- List the skills and experience you need to get the job done right.
- Decide if it will be full-time, part-time, or contract work.

WRITE A JOB DESCRIPTION

- Give your ad an active title that captures the essence of the role: "Seeking savvy self-starter to supervise sales for event promotion business," for example.
- Describe the role and its responsibilities in three to five sentences.
- Tell prospective employees a bit about your venture.
- Include years of experience required (if any) for the role.
- Include information on applying. What's required—resume, work samples, and references? How will candidates submit an application—via email, an online platform, or in person? When is your deadline?

COMPENSATION & BENEFITS

- Will you pay hourly, a salary, or by the project?
- Will you offer commission or bonuses?
- Can you offer benefits, such as paid time off, medical or dental insurance, or professional development?
- Will you pay weekly, biweekly, or monthly?
- Will you offer equity or revenue share in the company as compensation?
- Be sure to check legal obligations regarding compensation and benefits, as certain aspects are dictated by state and federal laws.

ADVERTISE

Promote via your website, social media, and email

Post on *LinkedIn*, *Indeed*, and other online job boards

Put up a sign at your retail or event location

Don't forget word-of-mouth—share with friends, family, and customers

INTERVIEW TIPS

THEY DIDN'T TEACH YOU IN SCHOOL

Now that you know how to define the roles you need to fill, write a job description, and attract applications, you'll have to interview candidates! Here's everything you'll need to know.

SCREEN APPLICATIONS

Set aside time to review applications, comparing them to the job requirements. Choose candidates you'd like to interview.

CONDUCT INTERVIEWS

Consider a fifteen- to thirty-minute phone screening to filter the right applicants for in-person interviews.

ASK THE RIGHT QUESTIONS

Ask open-ended questions that encourage a candidate to make a compelling case for the job.

- Walk me through your resume.
- Why are you interested in this role?
- What have you learned from previous positions that you could put to use in this role?

- What do you think will be the hardest thing about this job? Why?
- What's the best piece of feedback you've ever received? Why?
- Tell me about a team situation that didn't go well. What happened, and how did you help resolve it?

DON'T ASK

There are certain questions you can't ask in an interview. These include:

- What is your religious or political affiliation?
- How old are you?
- Are you married?
- Are you pregnant or planning to become pregnant?
- Do you have children?
- What is your race, color, or ethnicity?
- Are you disabled?
- Are you in debt?
- Do you drink or smoke?

LISTEN CAREFULLY

- Take notes during the interview so that you can review later.
- Be sure to leave time for your candidate to ask questions. It's a red flag if he or she doesn't have any!

CHECK REFERENCES

- Don't skip this part! Call your candidate's references to verify the dates and details of previous employment. Be sure to ask if, given the chance, that person would hire your candidate again.
- If your candidate looks good on paper but there's just something you can't put your finger on, try to figure this out via references.

MAKE AN OFFER

- Prepare an offer that includes compensation, pay periods, and benefits.
- Call your candidate and make the offer. Expect negotiation.
- Give your candidate time to decide— twenty-four to forty-eight hours is standard.
- Determine a start date.

AFTER THE HIRE

Be sure to contact each person you interviewed in person to tell them the position has been filled.

USE SCHEDULING TOOLS

Planning a meeting? Nothing is less fun than sending potential times back and forth in a never-ending email string. Use Doodle polls or tools like Calendly to simplify scheduling for everyone and, once a consensus is reached, generate calendar invitations to hold the time.

ONBOARD NEW CLIENTS

From proposal to scope of work to non-disclosure agreement (NDA), ensure you provide your client with everything he or she will need to know about working with you. Establish when and how you'll be paid, and submit any paperwork the client requires to pay you.

THE BUSINESS OF YOUR BUSINESS:

EXCEL AT CLIENT MANAGEMENT

Whether you're in creative services, consulting, or coaching, you're going to be asked one question over and over again by prospective clients or customers: what's your process? This means they want to know, **"How do you make the magic happen?"**

Of course, when you're first starting out, you might not have a ready answer yet. As you develop your ideas and build your business, be mindful of developing a repeatable and predictable process that can help you work efficiently—and close with clients.

CREATE AND MAINTAIN A TIMELINE

Use Google Docs, Basecamp, or another project management tool to create and track key dates for projects, even if they seem simple at the outset. You'll protect your own ability to deliver work on time if you're waiting for something that's actually your client's responsibility.

PROVIDE MATERIAL IN ADVANCE

No one works well on the fly. Send an agenda one to two days before the meeting that clearly captures its purpose and discussion points. Asking for someone's input or approval? Be sure to send files for review before the meeting.

DEVELOP A CLOSEOUT CHECKLIST

Use these tips to make wrapping up your project a dream.

- ☑ Ask for approval in writing, if applicable
- ☑ Express your gratitude for the opportunity
- ☑ Inquire about additional opportunities for collaboration
- ☐ Provide your final invoice before file delivery or your final meeting
- ☐ Ask for a testimonial and permission to use it
- ☐ Ask for consideration for future referrals

SECURITY CONCERNS

Managing risk and protecting your business
entails understanding the possible threats you
might face, from cybersecurity to the specter
of physical violence or property damage

INFORMATION SECURITY

How are you going to protect your proprietary information? When it comes to hacking concerns, you'll want to think carefully about what you have, where you store it, and how to protect it. Do limit use of public networks, back up your files daily, and use password protection (with a strong password) when possible.

Dealing with an incident

- Determine how your information was breached. Start by calling your Internet and website hosting providers to enlist their help. If resources allow, consider hiring a security consultant.

- You are legally required to inform customers if their information was breached.

- Prioritize creating an incident response plan to handle any future occurrences.

DID YOU KNOW?

No matter your location, the EU's GDPR (General Data Protection Regulation) could affect your business. Be sure you do your homework and know the facts!

PERSONNEL SECURITY

Sadly, employee abuse and workplace violence incidents do happen. While you cannot anticipate every possible scenario, you should thoroughly screen potential employees. Be sure to stay attuned to changes in behavior and handle any made threats with immediate action.

Dealing with an incident

- Call 911 or security immediately.

- Assist victims with prompt medical attention.

- Reach out to your lawyer right away.

PHYSICAL SECURITY

Protecting your property and your workplace is paramount. Locks, security systems, keycard access, closed-circuit televisions, and other measures—including sprinkler systems and fire alarms—are often necessary for office or retail establishments.

Dealing with an incident

- Report the matter to the police.

- Provide access to any video footage or other relevant evidence.

- Determine if customer information was breached— see Information Security.

- Assess additional security measures to protect yourself from future burglaries.

REGULATION & GOVERNANCE

Most small business regulation in the US falls into the following six categories:

1 ADVERTISING

Every US business is required to comply with the truth-in-advertising laws and could face lawsuits for violations. What does this mean?

- Advertising must be truthful and not misleading.

- Businesses must be prepared to back up any claims made in advertisements.

- Advertisements must be fair to competitors and consumers.

- Packaged goods must bear product information labels.

2 EMPLOYMENT & LABOR

Employment laws cover aspects of:

- Minimum wage.
- Benefits.
- Safety, health compliance, and working conditions.
- Work for non-US citizens.
- Equal opportunity employment.
- Privacy conditions.

3 ENVIRONMENTAL IMPACT

The Environmental Protection Agency regulates businesses' carbon footprints and their effects on the environment, and often works alongside state agencies.

4 PRIVACY PROTECTION

Sensitive information is collected from employees and customers during hiring and transactions. Privacy laws prevent businesses from disclosing this information, and people can sue your business if it violates them.

5 SAFETY & HEALTH

The Occupational Safety and Health Act of 1970 ensures that employers provide safe and sanitary work environments. If you're an employer, your business may be subject to inspections and a grading scale.

6 GOVERNANCE

Governance relates to how your business makes decisions and accomplishes oversight. If you're a sole proprietorship, governance is up to you and you alone. If you're an S corp, you'll have shareholders (even if singular—you) and must file an annual report with the state in which you operate.

GROWTH & SCALE

When you put in hard work, smart planning, and consistent effort, your business grows. Although you're at the beginning of this journey, you should already be thinking about growth and scale. When your business can serve a growing customer base without increasing overhead, you'll be on a healthy—and profitable—growth trajectory.

BE PROACTIVE

Anticipate customer demand instead of reacting to it. As you deliver products, sell services, or forge new business partnerships, you'll want to think about how to replicate what you're doing in the most efficient way possible. That might be as simple as creating and sticking to a defined process.

AVOID BOTTLENECKS & DEPENDENCIES

Just imagine: if everything had to go through you forever, you'd be the bottleneck. **Build a business with a mind toward reducing dependencies on particular people or parts of the process.** Consider subcontracting with people to whom you can teach your process. Use automation when possible.

FOCUS & SIMPLIFY

Offering a defined set of products or services lets you really focus on doing what you do best. Instead of chasing every project under the sun, you might offer three services. Rather than coaching anyone who needs it, you develop a niche. It all goes back to defining your ideal customers and creating products they love.

STEP BACK TO SEE THE BIG PICTURE

When you're starting out, every project or sale feels like the one that will sustain you. As you continue to build, though, you start to create a wave that sustains your business. **Eventually, you'll be big enough that your business will sustain itself, no matter who is in charge**—as long as that person is responsible, savvy, and willing to contribute the energy to succeed.

APPENDIX

US RESOURCES

US Department of Labor
1-866-4-USA-DOL
(1-866-487-2365)
www.dol.gov

The US DOL handles labor and employment: their site covers topics ranging from disability resources to information on required health plans and benefits, to information on employing minors. This is a good place to start.

You can also find state-specific resources on the site: www.dol.gov/oasam/programs/osdbu/state.htm.

Internal Revenue Service
1-800-829-4933
www.irs.gov/businesses/small-businesses-self-employed

The IRS's Small Business and Self-Employed Tax Center has forms, information, and other resources for small businesses. The IRS also assigns tax ID numbers for businesses.

US Small Business Administration (SBA)
SBA Answer Desk:
1-800-827-5722

ASL Consumer Support Line's
Contact Representative (videophone):
1-855-440-4960
www.sba.gov

This organization is aimed at providing small business owners with support and resources, including financing, education and information, and advocacy. Their business guide lays out the basic questions you need to consider to keep your business legally compliant.

Occupational Safety and Health
Administration (OSHA)
1-800-321-6742
www.osha.gov

The Occupational Safety and Health Administration (OSHA) is a part of the US Department of Labor and handles workplace safety. Check out their resources for information about keeping your workplace safe.

Service Corps of Retired Executives
1-800-634-0245
www.score.org

SCORE is a nonprofit that offers mentors, advice, business tools, and workshops for entrepreneurs.

US Patent and Trademark Office
1-800-786-9199
www.uspto.gov

Contact this department to set up trademarks (for things like your logo or business name) or patents (if your business involves a new invention).

Export.gov
www.export.gov

Export.gov, which is run by the US Department of Commerce's International Trade Administration (ITA), has market data, business tools, and advice for doing business internationally.

Small Business Development Centers (SBDC)
www.americassbdc.org

There are more than 1,000 SBDC offices throughout the US, and all of them offer free consulting services on the local level. They can connect entrepreneurs with funding resources, help with legal and accounting questions, and provide executive training sessions.

AUSTRALIAN RESOURCES

Australian Government—Business
www.business.gov.au

This online resource has basic information about running your business, from business plan to opening day. It also has links to grant and assistance resources, and info on taxes and other financial questions.

Australian Business License and Information
Service (ABLIS)
https://ablis.business.gov.au

This organization handles state, local, territory, and national business rules and regulations.

IP Australia
1300 65 10 10
www.ipaustralia.gov.au

This organization administers intellectual property rights and manages patents and trademarks. Visit their site to search existing IPs and to register your own trademarks, designs, or other intellectual property.

CANADIAN RESOURCES

Canadian Chamber of Commerce–
Tools for Small Business
www.chamber.ca/resources/
tools-for-small-business/

This is Canada's largest business association. They provide political advocacy for businesses. Their small business resource page provides information about business training resources, administration, finances, and human resources.

Canada Business
https://canadabusiness.ca/government/
regulations/regulated-business-activities/
human-resources-regulations/

You can find information on how to register your business, and learn about business rules and regulations, at the official Canada Business site.

You can find local regulations through your province's Ministry of Labor website.

Government of Canada–Business
www.canada.ca/en/services/business/start
.html

The Business category of the official Canadian government website walks you through the basics of starting a business in Canada: it has basic information about planning your business, along with links to government resources. There is also information on how to register your business; apply for any necessary permits and licenses; and find support and financing.

Innovation, Science, and Economic
Development Canada
www.ic.gc.ca

This agency offers a wealth of advice and information to Canadian entrepreneurs, from research and statistics to finding necessary business licenses and permits.

INDIAN RESOURCES

Ministry of Corporate Affairs (MCA)
www.mca.gov.in

The MCA handles the regulations and laws related to business in India. Their site has links to resources you need to set up your business, including links to get your business started and registered, and information about paying taxes.

Income Tax Department
www.incometaxindia.gov.in

On this site you can find specific tax laws and rules, information on paying taxes as a non-resident, and many more links to tools and information to get your taxes in order.

Ministry of Micro, Small, & Medium Enterprises
(MSME)
https://msme.gov.in

The MSME handles the rules and regulations related to micro, small, and medium businesses in India.

UK RESOURCES

Gov.UK Business and Self-Employed Page
www.gov.uk/browse/business

Gov.UK is the best place to start for any official government information, and their page on business has links to all the information you need, from advice on starting a business and tax details, to industry-specific rules and regulations (food handling, farming, childcare) and links for registering for trademarks and copyrights.

Her Majesty's Revenue and Customs (HMRC)
www.gov.uk/government/organisations/hm-
revenue-customs

You can find all the necessary tax information, including information on payroll, VAT, national insurance and more, at the HMRC page.

INDEX

ABOUT THE DESIGNER

Carissa Lytle is a marketer-turned-designer who loves creating infographics because of the way they beautifully meld typography, illustration, and design. She studied marketing at DePaul University and visual communication design at the School of the Art Institute of Chicago before starting out on her own as a freelance graphic designer. Fast-forward fifteen years and she now owns the award-winning, full-service design firm Right Angle Studio. Alongside her husband, Patrick—a former chief marketing officer—the pair balance creative insight and marketing know-how to run their business like a well-oiled machine. When they aren't collaborating on their clients' latest project, you can find them enjoying their free time with their four young daughters in the picturesque lakefront town of Highland Park on Chicago's North Shore.

ABOUT THE AUTHOR

Jara Kern tapped her entrepreneurial streak as a kindergartner, when she wrote to Hasbro with the idea for a new line of My Little Pony toys, accompanied by names, marketing copy, and detailed illustrations. While she's moved on from My Little Ponies, her knack for organizing ideas and expressing them in sparkling copy has stayed with her—and helped her nurture a thriving career. When she's not strategizing or writing, you'll find her running trails or learning about birds and bugs with her three children. She holds a degree in music performance from the Oberlin Conservatory of Music and an MBA from the University of Wisconsin-Madison.